THE HEBREW ALPHABET

Pronunciation and Writing Exercises

Book 1

א
ALEF

to

▪
YOD

Silvia C. Owley

R | E

Royally Educated

North Port, Florida

THE HEBREW ALPHABET—Book 1
Pronunciation and Writing Exercises

Copyright © 2024 Royally Educated, LLC

Published by Royally Educated, LLC
North Port, Florida
Email: royallyeducated@gmail.com

Hebrew Letters and Fonts designed by Silvia C. Owley

Unless otherwise indicated, Bible quotations are taken from the Hebrew WEB
(Hebrew World English Bible), an unrestricted free posting on the internet and a
public domain, updated revision of the American Standard Version of 1901.

Cover and Interior Design by Imagine!® Studios
www.ArtsImagine.com

Cover Image: EvgeniyBobrov/stock.adobe.com

ISBN: 979-8-9896128-0-2

First Royally Educated, LLC printing: January 2024

TABLE OF CONTENTS

AUTHOR'S NOTE

This has been an exciting journey studying the Hebrew language. English, Spanish and French are necessary languages to live in this world, but Hebrew is the apple of GOD's eye. As I was searching for the right introduction to GOD's beloved language, I stumbled upon a song that expressed GOD's love for humanity, well known today as **"The Love of GOD"** by F.M. Lehman, 1917. The more I dug into it, the more I realized that this was my LORD's choice to introduce His 10 Commandments in this workbook.

In my research, I found that in the 11th century, a poem entitled **"AKDAMUT MILIN"**, or **"Praises for GOD"**, were Jewish prayers used often in ancient worship by religious Jews that would inspire their personal writings. During the Festival of Weeks, a celebration of GOD giving Moses the 10 Commandments, the Jews read aloud this poem before reciting the 10 Commandments as it was the "Introductory words to reading the 10 Divine Commands". In the Jewish Prayer Book, the second stanza read:

> "At GOD's command is infinite power
> Which words cannot define.
> Were all the reeds pens and all the oceans ink,
> And all who dwell on earth scribes
> GOD's grandeur could not be told."

A German Jewish poet of the eleventh century, Rabbi Meir Ben Isaac Nehoral wrote his own poem, probably inspired by the "AKDAMUT MILIN", and later it was used for the song "The Love of GOD". At the end of his life, in an insane asylum cell in Germany, after being put to death, scrawled on the walls were found the words of Rabbi Meir Ben Isaac Nehoral:

> "Could we with ink the ocean fill
> And were the skies of parchment made;
> Were ev'ry stalk on earth a quill,
> And ev'ry man a scribe by trade;
> To write the love of GOD, above
> Would drain the ocean dry;
> Nor could the scroll contain the whole,
> Tho' stretched from sky to sky".

How ironic that these words represent the wholeness of "The Love of GOD" and the original "Praises for GOD" were said before reading the 10 Commandments, as this entire workbook is all about.

FOREWORD

By Jean Rosse

In Silvia Owley's new book, *THE HEBREW ALPHABET*, you will learn amazing insight into the depth of the mysteries hidden in the Hebrew language.

This workbook is like nothing else available for those who want to learn more about the roots of the Judeo-Christian faith contained in the powerful wisdom of the Hebrew letters.

Engaging, inspiring, thought-provoking and faith-building. You will find it so interesting; as you are learning revelations of GOD, you discover you are learning the basics of the Hebrew alphabet—almost effortlessly.

Jean Rosse holds a Bachelor of Science degree from Liberty University and has been a serious student of the Bible for over 30 years.

INTRODUCTION

Learning Hebrew is a divine challenge that many people have ventured into with teachers, pastors or by themselves.

The materials on the market are geared for those who already have a good basic knowledge of the Hebrew language. But acquiring a strong and solid foundation in this language is a real challenge.

I have been a foreign language teacher for over 40 years, using unconventional teaching methodologies to satisfy the basic prerequisites needed to teach a foreign language thoroughly.

As a teacher of English, Spanish and French for students of every level, age group, diverse social and economic backgrounds and nationalities, I have had to sow new seeds of enlightenment. In order to help my students understand the grammatical intricacies that are part of a language and relate them to their own language they must have an understanding of their own language structure first before learning another language.

So, creating new teaching techniques for my students is a challenging endeavor, which I enjoy immensely and have for many years.

In 2014, I went to a Messianic Christian church in Las Vegas, and became captivated by the old (new to me) Hebrew traditions that amazed me and hooked me instantly. I thought: *What an incredible way to get closer to THE LORD, since these are a shadow of the things to come.*

Observing and learning as much as I could, I was intrigued when I found out that my church could not read nor write Hebrew.

So I took it upon myself to try and learn Hebrew any way I could. I called local Jewish churches to sign up for Hebrew classes, but to no avail; they would not teach me because I was not Jewish. I searched the libraries for Hebrew books that would teach the basics, surfed the web, but was not satisfied as I could not get started with the basics.

I bought a Hebrew-English dictionary and had to get a magnifying glass to be able to see the Hebrew letters with their little dots and lines. I also became more confused when I read the meanings of Hebrew words in English as this required an English sounding transliteration (how a word is read and sounds) that aggravated the problem even more.

I realized that this task was going to be difficult, and I finally asked THE LORD to help me. Day by day, step by step, He directed me His way: to get familiar with the very basics, the alphabet. So, for six months I memorized the Hebrew alphabet, letter by letter, writing it, pronouncing it (challenging myself even at night to visualize each letter of the alphabet), then relating each letter to words that began with that letter. As I kept questioning THE LORD endlessly on "why this, why that", He showed me—He opened the eyes of my understanding like never before.

These Hebrew lessons do not follow the traditional teachings of Judaism or Rabbinical theories, nor is it Aramaic. These are the down loads of the Holy Spirit into my spirit focusing on the Word of God, the Torah—the very first words THE LORD dictated to Moses in the first 5 Books of the Bible.

To learn the Hebrew letters intimately is to delve into the origins, the roots, and the formation of each letter that births a word reminding us how our LORD became the Living Word.

It is a privilege and an honor to teach anyone who hungers and thirsts for HIS pure Word as we uncover new fresh meanings of Scripture.

May you enjoy these lessons as much as I am delighting in dipping into this bottomless source of knowledge of our LORD. His Word is as deep as the deepest oceans and is there for us to drink!

Methodology

As I began to learn to read Hebrew in 2014, and knew just enough to sound out a Hebrew word into English, I saw that the translation given in English was not what was written in Hebrew. This really perturbed me. I thought that the words from the Scriptures in English were always an "accurate translation" from the Hebrew. If mistranslations have been passed down for centuries to us, then how far off is the Scripture we are studying and learning from what THE LORD meant?

This is when I realized that it was of utmost importance to learn the Hebrew letters thoroughly, with THE LORD's help and guidance, by studying one letter at a time and putting on Moses' sandals as when he received his teachings from God. By recognizing each letter, by sounding it out through the help of *super fast CDs*, I could read Hebrew while comparing with the English transliteration. By following along these simple principles, I established a firm base for reading while creating new rules generating from my foreign language teaching experiences.

The first change I made was to use my Spanish teaching techniques for pronunciation in order to read Hebrew phonetically, without getting entangled with the English vowel (a, e, i, o, u) sounds. I adopted the Spanish vowel sounds and the French consonant sounds to be as close as possible to a Jewish speaker. This has been very helpful for not getting confused with the English vowel sounds transliterated in the dictionaries.

VOWEL SOUNDS:

a = ah	**e** = eh	**i** = ee	**o** = oh	**u** = oo
car	get	cheese	for	poor
casa	perro	lindo	Sonora	mucho

CONSONANT SOUNDS:

Y = ia	**r** =	French throat sound Spanish tongue sound	**th** = t	**ph** = p

HEBREW SOUNDS:

k = kh, k, q   **h** = h, silent at end of word

ts = ts, tz

Simplicity of the Spanish Vowels

Simplicity, as THE LORD has always taught, is the key to better understanding and quicker learning.

The advantage that I have as a foreign language teacher of 40 years is to have understood the depths of certain languages, their grammar, their spelling and pronunciation rules, and "now" be able to draw out the similarities and blend them into the Hebrew pronunciation. English speaking countries have Hebrew-English dictionaries with English transliteration/pronunciation. Each country has its own transliteration or ways to pronounce Hebrew using the sounds of their native language. I saw a Hebrew prayer with Russian transliteration written for Russians; this is the way Russians will pronounce Hebrew words with their native accent.

I noticed that Jews speak Hebrew using French consonant sounds and Spanish vowel sounds.

So it was natural to choose Spanish as the cleanest and easiest way for pronouncing the Hebrew vowels. Spanish has 5 vowels and only 5 vowel sounds; English has 42 vowel sounds with only 5 vowels.

So, if you have never studied Spanish or French, memorize the charts above and the Hebrew alphabet as this will speed up letter recognition and you will begin to read Hebrew words.

Writing In Hebrew

Writing the Hebrew letters has also been simplified as there are many fonts to choose from. Choosing the simplest and clearest font makes it possible for us to imitate each letter. All you need is to copy exactly the examples in the book. If one tittle, one little line of ⅛ of an inch is missing or added on, another letter is created.

Our goal is to be able to read passages of the Torah (Bible) in Hebrew, and understand each others' Hebrew writings. If one letter is off by just a little, we will drift into another letter. *Being in one mind and one accord* is THE LORD's encouragement.

There is a golden rule that the Scribes followed and that we will respect as well as it makes it easier to read what we wrote. Each Hebrew letter is clearly separated from the next letter. They never touch each other. Each letter is a container loaded with THE LORD's power/powder/life of creation infused into each letter. **Hebrews 11:3** says *"By faith, we understand that the universe has been framed by the word of God"*. Letters unite to create what we speak. Hebrew words are the most powerful words in the universe as they are linked directly to THE LORD's heart. Watch what you say even with lesser words.

A friend purchased for me, in Israel, a beautiful Hebrew-French Torah. Since the print was quite small, and the Hebrew letters had been shrunk too, I had to read the Hebrew letters with a magnifying glass to discern the vowel points, and to distinguish between certain letters because some bled onto the other letter.

Consonants and Vowel Points

I always feel honored to write THE LORD's letters. It is having the Head CEO of the Universe oversee your work, and encourage you to get closer to HIM because of your LOVE for HIM and for making the time to learn HIS language. The Holy Spirit is very present whenever you study Hebrew! You will experience this!

You will be introduced to the accents/vowel points. As a language teacher I noted that the accents in Hebrew are not consistent with the stress that a letter should carry. One time a letter carries an accent that is emphasized, another time that same accent is not emphasized. At this point, we are just learning to say the word in Hebrew, and the accents will come at a later time.

Hebrew has consonants (b, c, d, f . . .) like our language, but the vowels are mostly created by dots and/or dashes. The silent letters like the A (**ALEF** and **AYIN**) can take any vowel accent (a, e, i, o, u) and make it sound like ELOHIM though it starts with the letter A.

Many Hebrew words in books and even in the Torah do not have the written accents/vowel points, so it becomes very challenging to find the word in the dictionary and know how to pronounce it correctly with the right vowel.

Nevertheless we will study the different accents or vowel points a letter can carry so when we read a word in Hebrew we will be able to sound it out correctly.

Respect for THE LORD's Letters

When writing a Hebrew word into the English alphabet (transliterating) every letter will be capitalized because each letter in Hebrew is important to THE LORD. When we translate from the Hebrew we do not need to use capital letters when writing into English.

DEFINITION OF TERMS

Phonetic sound: a system of written symbols that represent speech sounds so it is as close as possible to the way it actually sounds.

Phonetics: Study of speech sounds (used in 1836).

Example: David is phonetically spelled in the English dictionary:

Dāhveed   Da-wid

Diacritic: a mark placed over, under, through a letter to show how the letter should be pronounced, or a phonetic character indicating a phonetic value different from an unmarked one.

French example: déjà vu—uses two diacritics (used first in 1866)

Translation: words changed from one language into a different language.

The sun = el sol   ELOHIM = GOD, Gods, god, gods

Transliteration: to write words or letters in the characters of another alphabet depending on who the translator is:

HANNUKAH, CHANUKA, KHANUKA, JANUKA, JANUKHA . . .

Studying Hebrew must be made easy and simple. Doing away with English phonetics will alleviate most of the problem for spelling, reading and writing Hebrew.

UNDERSTANDING THE BASICS OF THE HEBREW LETTERS

THE FIRST 10 LETTERS, ALEF (א) TO YOD (י)

Relating the Old Testament to the Letters of the Alphabet

The First 10 Hebrew letters relate to the Old Testament.

Amazingly, each Hebrew letter corresponds with the precise order of the 10 Commandments in Hebrew.

Reconciling with the Past—the Beginnings

To become successful in knowing and recognizing each letter of the Hebrew alphabet, you need to re-write each letter on your exercise page in this book following the study of that letter.

As you write the letter, say its name, what sound it makes. (**B** as in **b**ook, **B** as in **BEN** (son), #2, and remember its number.

Each Hebrew word begins with a specific letter of the alphabet. The most common words associated with that letter have been chosen to associate it with that letter (**B** as in **BORE** = **Creator**).

THE LORD'S Directives for Mankind . . . Writing from Right to Left ←

Civilization began in the East. There are many examples of GOD's creation that took place in the Orient. Whenever Jews build a church or Temple they consider the longitudinal axis pointing east with the chief altar located at the east end; the wall of the Synagogue faces east; in prayer, the Jews face east when in Diaspora (Jews living outside of the homeland); the Tabernacle's entrance faces east; the sun rises on the east; the garden of Eden was planted in the east; the Cherubim are stationed on the east side of the garden of Eden; in Ezekiel's vision, GOD's glory comes from the east and enters the temple from the east; this temple faces east with a river floating east from it; the scriptures say to face the east when addressing GOD, and the west when addressing the enemy. The world turns horizontally using the four cardinal points ⊕ to direct us on this earth.

In Hebrew, YEMIN means right side. It is considered to be the strong side; the right leg and eye are favored in strength.

> As far as the east is from the west, so far has he removed our transgressions from us. **(Psalm 103: 12)**

GOD begins to forgive us from the east where HE resides, then continues east all the way around the world to clean us up perfectly and entirely from sin.

North is considered the basis for the compass. If we face north, our right hand faces east. Spiritually we are sitting at the right hand of YASHUA, as He is sitting at the right hand of His Father, ABA*.

ABA is looking down on us. GOD's Residence is vertical. ↑ He lives in the spirit world. ↗

> I lay in Zion for a foundation a stone, . . . a precious cornerstone **(Isaiah 28:16)**

Justice is the measuring line; **righteousness** the plumb line.

We are beginning the study of the Hebrew letters focusing on the first five books of the Bible, the TORAH. In those days THE LORD was directing and instructing mankind through Prophets, and Kings. People did not have a personal relationship with the Messiah before the New Testament, so it was more with fear and trembling that they worshipped GOD-ELOHIM.

For this reason—looking up to GOD ↑, bowing down, looking down ↘, praising (up) Him ✋ will be the order of respect to GOD in the letters of the Old Testament. These Hebrew letters will be written from **bottom to top**, as an act of worship and praise to our LORD, and for showing our total dependency on THE LORD in the Old Testament.

---

*   Greek and English spellings are ABBA. Hebrew spelling only has one B.

THE LORD is instructing us from HIS throne, from the **right side to the left side**.

REMEMBER in the Old Testament!

- Use a pencil with a good eraser.

- Do not allow each letter in a word to touch each other.

- Write from Right to Left. ←

- Write from Bottom to Top. ↑

- Memorize the letter, its sound, its number.

  B , #2

- Memorize one or two words that stand out with that letter. This is a suggestion for memorizing:

  B as in **BARA = to create**   **BIER = destroyed**

Lesson 1

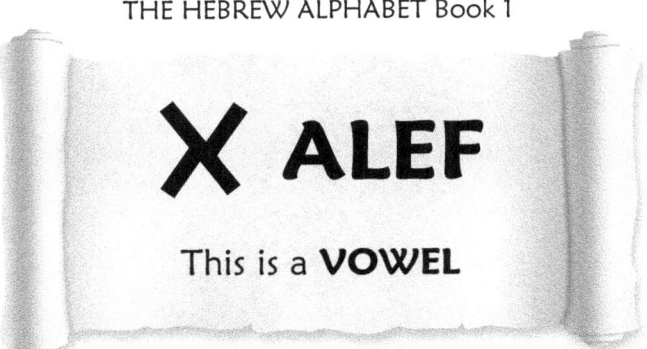

א ALEF

This is a **VOWEL**

Example of letter in a calligraphic style

PRACTICE AND MEMORIZE: ◄ WRITE HEBREW FROM RIGHT TO LEFT ◄

Example

Practice

Example of vowel sounds with a specific diacritic mark: short vowels

a   **e**   **i**   **o**   **u**

SOME WORDS STARTING WITH א :

Dad	**ABA**
GOD	**EL**
Love	**AHAVA**
GOD (Trinity)	**ELOHIM**
Man, Red	**ADAM**
Faith, Surely	**AMEN**
One	**EKHAD**
Faith	**EMUNA**

NOTES:

THE 1ST COMMANDMENT

'I am Yahweh . . . You shall have no other gods before me' (**Exodus 20: 2, 3**)

ALEF (**X**): The 1st letter in a word is the most important letter as it depicts how GOD portrays that word in His Divine order of Creation. In the 1st Commandment, the ALEF begins with the names of GOD: **E**L (GOD), **E**LOHIM (GODS, gods), **A**BA (FATHER), **A**VI (my DAD).

The 10th letter of the Hebrew alphabet, **YOD** (**'**) is also the 10th Commandment. The Personal Names of THE LORD begin with that letter: **YA**, **Y**HVH (**YA**HWE), **YA**SHUA (Jesus). **YA** is GOD's Family Name.

Throughout the 10 Commandments, each respective letter of the alphabet will begin that commandment using the first letter in the alphabet. This is a great way to remember the 10 Commandments once and for all. Also learning a positive and negative word in Hebrew beginning with the same letter helps memorize: Love versus Anger.

INTERESTING FACTS:

- The first 3 Commandments are dedicated to **GOD.**
- The following 2 Commandments target **Christians** to observe and to do.
- The last 5 Commandments speak to **mankind** and the unsaved world.

The two tablets of stone, received by Moses, and hand carved by THE LORD, are split. It shows a very clear separation of the world and His children who are made into His image.

In the Old Testament, the 1st Commandment says in **Deuteronomy 6:5**: *'and you shall love Yahweh your God with all your heart, and with all your soul, and with all your might.'* The 2nd, 3rd, 4th, and 5th commandments are to be kept by His children for the Love of GOD and for the love and respect of mankind—starting at the home, our foundation and roots, **our parents.**

In the New Testament, **Romans 13:10** says: *Love therefore is the fulfillment of the law.*

NOTES:

Practice the **ALEF** using the middle line.

X **X**

NOTES:

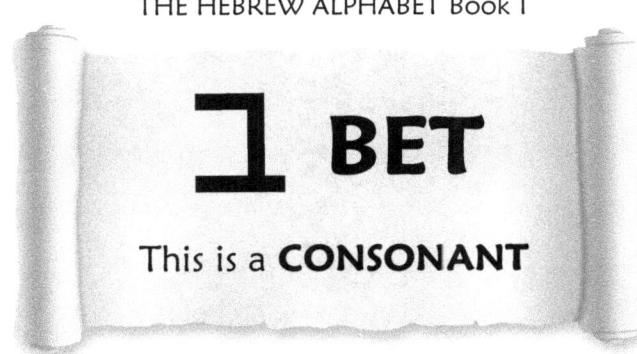

Lesson
2

⊐ BET

This is a **CONSONANT**

Example of letter in a calligraphic style

PRACTICE AND MEMORIZE: ◀ WRITE HEBREW FROM RIGHT TO LEFT ◀

Example

Practice

Example of vowel sounds with a specific diacritic mark: long vowels

| ba, va | be, ve | bi, vi | bo, vo | bu, vu |

SOME WORDS STARTING WITH ⊐:

Creator	**BORE**
Son	**BEN**
Morning	**BOKER**
Blessed	**BARUKH**
Good morning	**BOKER TOV**
He destroyed	**BIER**

Exercise: *Write the correct letters from Right to Left.*

Father, Dad   **ABA** (ALEF-BET-ALEF) _____

NOTES:

THE 2ᴺᴰ COMMANDMENT

*'You shall not make for yourselves an idol, nor any image of anything
. . . you shall not bow yourself down to them . . .'* (**Exodus 20:4, 5**)

The second letter, **BET** (‏ב‎), is focused on words such as *to build*, and *to construct*. THE LORD does not want us to create graven images to replace HIM.

In the Old Testament people built idols out of clay, carving them out of wood then bowing down before them, Afterwards they used the leftover materials as firewood to cook their meals. Any type of idol where mankind bows down to and worships is an abomination to THE LORD.

ELOHIM (GOD-Trinity) created all things by exhaling the word through THE WORD. The vowels are Life put into the consonants to give them substance as they became a WORD. Without these vowels the consonants are just clinging cymbals: btfl, btrfls, bntfl . . . but linked to a vowel they become "beautiful, butterflies, bountiful".

THE LORD's name is this Life.

Speaking, saying words create life, existence; these words are floating in space and have been for centuries.

> **BARUKH** = Blessed
>
> **BAAR** = Fool, Ignorant

That is why space needs serious cleaning, and it shall be . . .

NOTES:

Practice the **BET** using the middle line.

בּ ב

NOTES:

Lesson 3

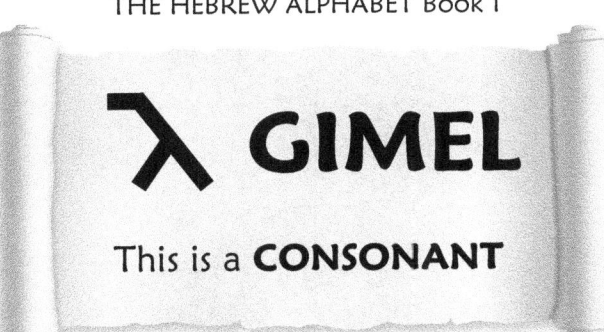

λ GIMEL

This is a **CONSONANT**

*Example of letter
in a calligraphic style*

PRACTICE AND MEMORIZE: ◄ WRITE HEBREW FROM RIGHT TO LEFT ◄

Example

Practice

Example of vowel sounds with a specific diacritic mark: long vowels

λ	λ	λ	λ	λ
ga	ge	gi	go	gu

SOME WORDS STARTING WITH λ :

Salvation	**GULA**
Redeemer	**GOEL**
Gentile	**GOI**
Body	**GUF**
Corpse	**GUFA**
Fool	**GOLEM**

Exercise: *Write the correct letters from Right to Left.*

Housetop   **GAG** (GIMEL-GIMEL) _____

NOTES:

THE 3RD COMMANDMENT

'You shall not take the name of Yahweh your God in vain . . .' (**Exodus 20:7**)

The first three commandments are addressing our LORD. He wants us to Love Him above anything else. He wants our total attention and commitment by putting away all idols and anything that takes us away from Him.

This third commandment addresses our words and our mouth. He does not want anything immoral coming out of our lips and in particular using His name in a profane manner. The Jews knew better!

Don't insult the Holy Spirit by careless words.

These first three commandments are THE LORD's sacred orders to us, His children as we are to keep proclaiming His HOLINESS.

GAVAH = Become high, tall

GAAVTAN = Vain

Respect begins with THE LORD, our only GOD. We are spiritual beings given an earthly body to live in this world. We live by Faith once we understand that ABA, our Heavenly Father created us a long time ago in HIM, and today we are here to testify of HIS LOVE for us. As we grasp these truths, we will begin to understand the depths of HIS NAME, HIS Grace, HIS Kindness and most important—HIS WORD—the Bible, our personal **Owner's Manual** for successful earth living until it's time to go Home.

NOTES:

Practice the **GIMEL** using the middle line.

ג ג

NOTES:

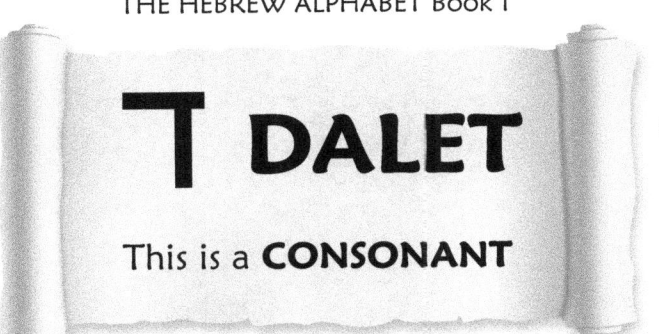

Lesson

4

⊤ DALET

This is a **CONSONANT**

Example of letter in a calligraphic style

PRACTICE AND MEMORIZE: ◄ WRITE HEBREW FROM RIGHT TO LEFT ◄

Example

Practice

Example of vowel sounds with a specific diacritic mark: short vowels

⊤	⊤	⊤	⊤	⊤
da	**de**	**di**	**do**	**du**

SOME WORDS STARTING WITH ⊤:

Door	**DELET**
Way, Via	**DEREKH**
Blood	**DAM**
To refuse, Put off	**DAKHA**
A judge	**DAYAN**
Imitation	**DEME**

Exercise: *Write the correct letters from Right to Left.*

Fish   **DAG** (DALET-GIMEL) _____

NOTES:

THE 4ᵀᴴ COMMANDMENT

'Remember the Sabbath* day, to keep it holy.' (**Exodus 20:8**)

When GOD wrote the Commandments with His finger, He meant it.

The 7th day (Saturday) is the only day mentioned in the Bible that GOD has specifically told us to observe it.

'God rested on the seventh day from all his works . . .' (**Hebrews 4:4**)

Notice the repetition of chapter 4, verse 4, and the 4th commandment.

WHY SATURDAY?

GOD rested from all His work of Creation, and chose this day to rest.

*God **blessed** the seventh day, and made it **holy**, because he rested in it from all his work which he had created and made.* (**Genesis 2:3**, emphasis added)

WHY SHOULD WE REST ALSO?

GOD set an example for us to follow. Our body needs rest, recuperation, renewal, restoration, re-evaluation, re-thinking, re-planning so we will receive our RE-WARD for obeying.

OUR REST—SHALOM

If we do not take time to rest, to relax and to renew ourselves, our life could be cut short, unable to fulfill GOD's plan for our lives.

The Israelites were smitten by GOD's anger because they did not rest and continued to work. Their disobedience of unbelief is a sin, and they did not enter into GOD's rest of trust and peace.

---

*   Greek and English spellings are SABBATH. Hebrew spelling only has one B, and since the TH is not pronounce it will be eliminated.

Today we self destruct under the leadership of Satan's work orders and accusations: *"do, do, do!—shame on you! You are not working hard enough, the poor people. You need to spend more time working for them! You're so selfish! Etc. . . ."* and then we really get sick from exhaustion which opens the door to many diseases and illnesses.

Do we live for GOD? Do we live to please ourselves or others?

The SHABAT day is **so** Holy and special to GOD that we will be highly blessed for believing what GOD declared: keeping it Holy, enjoying our rest in His fellowship, with family, doing what we like and not feeling guilty.

(See page 64 for the SHABAT prayer of Friday, at sunset.)

NOTES:

Practice the **DALET** using the middle line.

ד ד

NOTES:

Lesson 5

HE

This is a **CONSONANT** and a **VOWEL**

Example of letter in a calligraphic style

PRACTICE AND MEMORIZE: ◄ WRITE HEBREW FROM RIGHT TO LEFT ◄

Example

Practice

Example of vowel sounds with a specific diacritic mark: long vowels

ha	he	hi	ho	hu

SOME WORDS STARTING WITH ה:

Glory (beauty)	**HADAR**
To save, rescue	**HOSHIA**
To praise	**HILEL**
Mountain	**HAR**
He	**HU**

Exercise: *Write the correct letters from Right to Left.*

| Behold (see) | **HO, HA** (HE-ALEF) | _____ |
| Love | **AHAVA** (ALEF-HE-BET-HE) | _____ |

NOTES:

THE 5TH COMMANDMENT

'Honor your father and your mother . . .' (**Exodus 20:12**)

Respect for our parents is the foundation of society. When there is honor and obedience at home, there is order outside.

Society is based on what happens at home, how kindly, respectfully and lovingly children treat their parents.

Without love, respect and order there is chaos, violence and juvenile delinquency. Just look outside; it's everywhere.

With GOD, we are to respect HIM even more. As we obey the first 5 Commandments, we will avoid the chaos and anarchy of the next 5 Commandments.

This is why THE LORD **engraved this in stone**—for us to **obey** and **respect** our Heavenly Father and to listen and do what He has told us to do.

HIKSHIV = To accept advice or obey

HERAYON = Pregnancy

HAPALA = Abortion

NOTES:

Practice the **HE** using the middle line.

ה ה

NOTES:

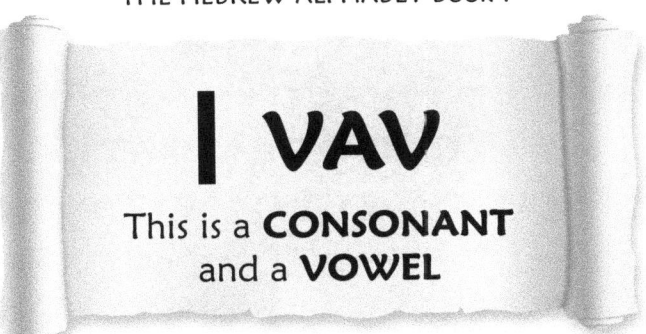

*Example of letter
in a calligraphic style*

Lesson 6

׀ VAV
This is a **CONSONANT**
and a **VOWEL**

PRACTICE AND MEMORIZE: ◄ WRITE HEBREW FROM RIGHT TO LEFT ◄

Example

Practice

Example of vowel sounds with a specific diacritic mark: long vowels

| va | ve | vi | vo* | vu* |

SOME WORDS STARTING WITH ׀:

Leviticus, Legislation	**VAYIKRA**
To verify, certify	**VIDE**
Certain	**VADAI**
And	**VA, VE**

---

* An extra VAV is added to the left of a letter to emphasize the long vowel. Before the addition of vowel points or accents, in the 10th century, there was an extra VAV that helped the reader put him on the right track of either an "O" or a "U".

Exercise: *Write the correct letters from Right to Left.*

Be   **HEVE** (HE-VAV-ALEF) _____

David   **DAVID** (DALET-VAV-DALET) _____

NOTES:

THE 6ᵀᴴ COMMANDMENT

'You shall not murder.' (**Exodus 20:13**)

The 6th Commandment is the beginning of GOD's intervention to guide mankind to live a civilized life, and not to self-destruct.

These next 5 Commandments aim at establishing order in a sinful world as GOD's children venture into a wolf-infested world ready to annihilate them.

Since the world does not want to hear the truth, it is becoming darker and darker; but we, the children of GOD are to become the Light in the midst of this obscurity and darkness.

Once again, if there is law and order, as the 5th Commandment suggests, there will be respect, love and peace.

VELAD = A newborn

VIDUI = Confession

NOTES:

Practice the **VAV** using the middle line.

NOTES:

Lesson 7

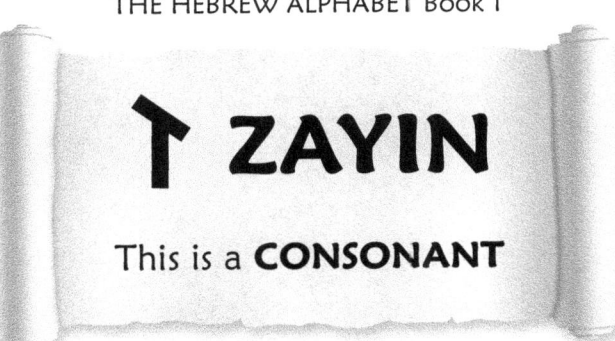

ז ZAYIN

This is a **CONSONANT**

Example of letter in a calligraphic style

PRACTICE AND MEMORIZE: ◀ WRITE HEBREW FROM RIGHT TO LEFT ◀

Example

Practice

Example of vowel sounds with a specific diacritic mark: long vowels

za	ze	zi	zo	zu

SOME WORDS STARTING WITH ז:

Purity	**ZAKUT**
Careful, cautious	**ZAHIR**
Prostitution	**ZNUT**
Infection	**ZIHUM**

Exercise: *Write the correct letters from Right to Left.*

Couple (a)   **ZUG** (ZAYIN-VAV-GIMEL) _____

Gold   **ZAHAV** (ZAYIN-HE-BET) _____

NOTES:

THE 7ᵀᴴ COMMANDMENT

'You shall not commit adultery.' (**Exodus 20:14**)

The next Commandment targets lust that is rampant nowadays in our world. It is everywhere. Our poor children are exposed to it wherever they go, on the billboards, in their movies, . . .

THIS 7ᵀᴴ COMMANDMENT BREAKS:

- 1ˢᵗ Commandment, Love.
- 5ᵗʰ Commandment, Honor and Respect to parents
- 6ᵗʰ Commandment, not to murder.

Lust (**IVA**) is the opposite of Love (**AHAVA**).

Lust is the opposite of Respect (**ZIA**).

Love is the opposite of rape (**ONES**).

An unwanted pregnancy leads to murder.

NOTES:

Practice the **ZAYIN** using the middle line.

ז   ז

NOTES:

Lesson

8

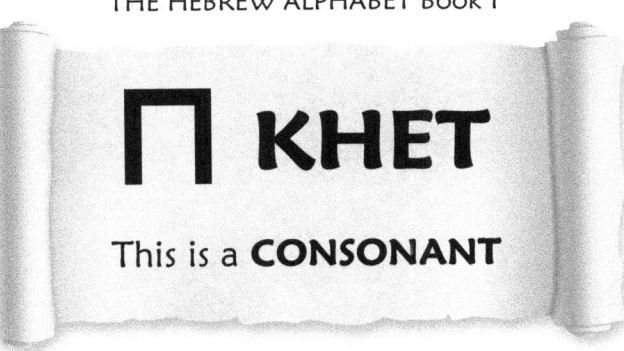

∏ KHET

This is a **CONSONANT**

Example of letter in a calligraphic style

PRACTICE AND MEMORIZE: ◄ WRITE HEBREW FROM RIGHT TO LEFT ◄

Example

Practice

Example of vowel sounds with a specific diacritic mark: long vowels

kha **khe** **khi** **kho** **khu**

SOME WORDS STARTING WITH ∏:

Wise, smart	**KHAKHAM**
Celebration	**KHAGIGA**
Sin	**KHET**
To desecrate	**KHILEL**
To lust, covet	**KHAMAD**

Exercise: *Write the correct letters from Right to Left.*

To celebrate   **KHAGAG** (KHET-GIMEL-GIMEL) _____

Alive   **KHAI** (KHET-YOD) _____

NOTES:

THE 8ᵀᴴ COMMANDMENT

'You shall not steal.' (**Exodus 20:15**)

By using wisdom you will avoid the future implications of what stealing brings. Be wise; don't be a fool.

We can blame the 5th Commandment for children not obeying their parents. But the parents are equally guilty—if not much more—for not establishing a close relationship with them. Today, many parents don't know what their children are doing, who their friends are and where they are. This secretive youth is submerged in their cell phones and computers with who knows who. They are shutting themselves off more and more to others, becoming anti-social, hateful and just guided by what society is saying on the internet. This is the generation of tomorrow!!!

So many children are left to themselves—not understanding what is right and what is wrong. As they grow up it is too late to discipline them; they are too big to be punished. Only the Law and the consequences of the Command-ments will do it.

> **KHAKHAM** = Wise, Smart
>
> **KHET** = Sin

NOTES:

Practice the **KHET** using the middle line.

ח ח

NOTES:

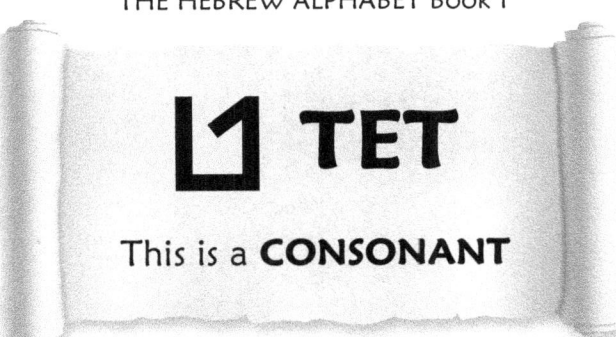

Lesson 9

Example of letter in a calligraphic style

PRACTICE AND MEMORIZE: ◄ WRITE HEBREW FROM RIGHT TO LEFT ◄

Example

Practice

Example of vowel sounds with a specific diacritic mark: short vowels

| ta | te | ti | to | tu |

SOME WORDS STARTING WITH ‏ט‎:

Ritual	**TEKES**
Body	**TORSO**
Error	**TAUT**

Exercise: *Write the correct letters from Right to Left.*

Virtue, goodness	**TUV** (TET-VAV-BET) _____
Good, fine	**TOV** (TET-VAV-BET) _____
Favor (a)	**TOVA** (TET-VAV-BET-HE) _____

NOTES:

THE 9TH COMMANDMENT

'You shall not give false testimony against your neighbor.' (**Exodus 20:16**)

As the degree of severity of each Commandment implicates the actions of the next Commandment, not telling the truth and lying about another person, it opens the door—though it seems harmless and rhetoric—to the father of lies, Satan. The Hebrew Bible, the Torah, only acknowledges the word "Satan". Devil is a Greek word that loses authority and power as it is a man-made word.

Habitual falsification of innocent people and/or facts is a sin that leads straight to hell. If he doesn't make a mental inventory of his life it will be too late . . . for eternity.

Repentance and turning back from a putrid life is only possible through YAS-HUA (Jesus). No matter how low, how bad and how evil one has lived his life it can all be made right by the last Commandment of the Old Testament.

TUV = Virtue

TAUT = Error

NOTES:

Practice the **TET** using the middle line.

NOTES:

Lesson 10

ˈ YOD

This is a **CONSONANT** and a **VOWEL**

Example of letter in a calligraphic style

PRACTICE AND MEMORIZE: ◀ WRITE HEBREW FROM RIGHT TO LEFT ◀

Example

Practice

Example of vowel sounds with a specific diacritic mark: long vowels

ya, ia	ye, ie	yi, i	yo, io	yu, iu

Exercise: *Write the correct letters from Right to Left.*

Jewish	**YEHUDI** (YOD-HE-VAV-DALET-YOD)

_____

To praise	**YADA** (YOD-DALET-HE) _____
Hand	**YAD** (YOD-DALET) _____
THE LORD	**YAHWE** (YOD-HE-VAV-HE) _____
Gentile	**GOI** (GIMEL-VAV-YOD) _____
Celebration	**KHAGIGA** (KHET-GIMEL-YOD-GIMEL-HE)

_____

NOTES:

THE 10ᵀᴴ COMMANDMENT

'You shall not covet your neighbor's house.' (**Exodus 20:17**)

This is the last Commandment of the Old Testament passed down from THE LORD to Moses and to us.

These 10 Commandments are for the well being of humanity, for order and for accountability.

ABA, our Heavenly Father, loves us so much that HE doesn't want to lose us, forever in hell, because of sin. HE sent YASHUA, Jesus, His Son to earth to be sacrificed and killed for us to fulfill the Jewish traditions that opened the door to forgiveness by shedding blood in exchange for being forgiven by GOD.

While He was on earth, YASHUA taught that only one thing mattered to our Heavenly Father, ABA, which is to love HIM with all of our being, and all else will fall into His divine plan.

Assuredly the only way to the Father is through the Son. YASHUA gave His life up, as an act of obedience to His/our Father as He sacrificed Himself for all of us.

By *asking GOD*, the Father **to forgive us for all of our sins** through YASH-UA's Blood on the cross, we are now clean, forgiven, and presentable before our Heavenly Father ABA. Now we can **invite YASHUA to enter into our hearts** and become **Our LORD** and **Our Savior**. We are now in GOD's care and protection forever with HIM.

This is the most important spiritual step of our lives since our next destination will be Heaven—and not hell. We are safe in Him.

GOD is **LOVE**, the 1ˢᵗ letter and 1ˢᵗ Commandment; **YA**SHUA is our LORD and Savior, the 10ᵗʰ letter and 10ᵗʰ Commandment. That SEALS the edicts of our Heavenly Father for us to come Home!

The Commandments are now summarized by YASHUA into two Commandments: **Love** THE LORD your GOD with all your heart, mind and soul, and also love your neighbor as yourself.

NOTES:

Practice the **YOD** using the middle line.

NOTES:

EXERCISES

1. Can you read the Hebrew words without peeking?

Underneath each Hebrew letter write the English corresponding letter. Then you will be able to read the Hebrew word from right to left. Rewrite the English letters from left to right, as normal. Finally, translate the Hebrew word into English.

גג   דג   יד   אבא
G D   D Y   A B A

YAD   **ABA**

Father

אחבב   יהד   דוד   חגג
     Ya   V   KH

KHAGAG

2. Can you write the Hebrew words, right to left, using the Hebrew alphabet?

My Father = **AVI** (ALEF-BET-YOD) _____

Good = **TOV** (TET-VAV-BET) _____

Hand = **YAD** (YOD-DALET) _____

3. Guess the Hebrew word.

Father = (ALEF-BET-ALEF) _____

Behold = (HE-ALEF) _____

THE LORD = (YOD-HE-VAV-HE) _____

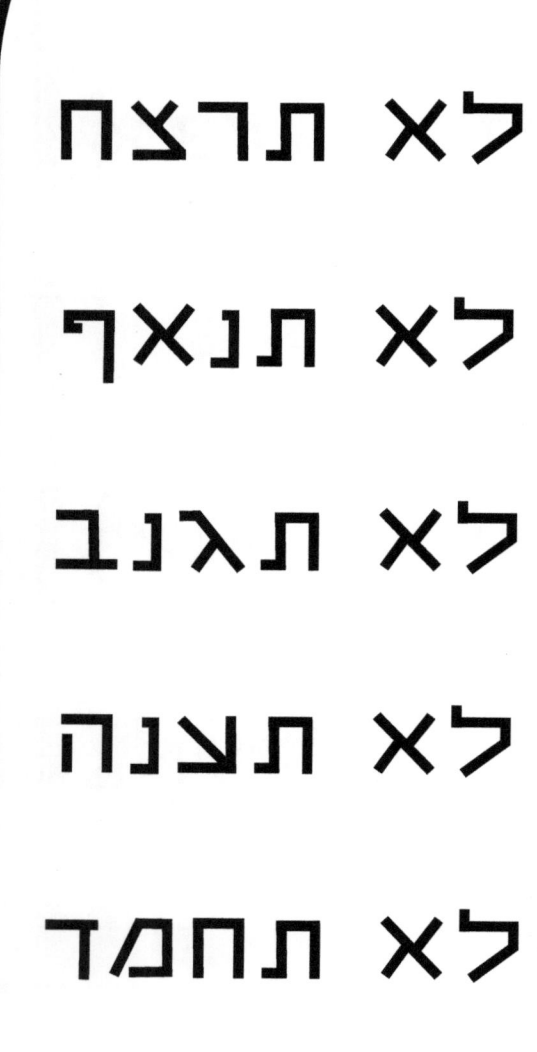

לא תרצח

לא תנאף

לא תגנב

לא תצנה

לא תחמד

אנכי ה'

לא יה'ה

לא תשא

זכור את

כבד את

LITERAL TRANSLATION OF THE 10 COMMANDMENTS TABLETS FROM HEBREW

GOD

I.	I (THE MOST) AM THE LORD	ANOKHI YAHWE
II.	WILL NOT HAVE	LO YIHYE
III.	NOT BEAR	LO TISA

CHRISTIANS

IV.	REMEMBER	ZAKHOR ET
V.	HONOR	KABED ET

MANKIND

VI.	NO KILLING	LO TIRTSAKH
VII.	NO ADULTERY	LO TINAP
VIII.	NO STEALING	LO TIGNOV
IX.	NO ANSWER	LO TAANE
X.	NO JEALOUSY	LO TAKHMOD

CELEBRATING THE SHABAT REST

The lady of the house lights the SHABAT candles as the sun is setting on Friday evening. This will vary according to the season. As the day is ending, she is welcoming the new day which starts when it is dark.

She lights the right candle first, then uses that candle to light the second candle.

She recites the following prayer:

Blessed are You, O LORD our GOD, King of the universe, who has sanctified us by Your commandments and commanded us to light the SHABAT candles.

It is Your will, LORD, my GOD, that You grace me and my husband, all my relatives and Christian friends, and give to us and to all of Israel a good and long life.

Remember us favorably. Bless us with plentiful blessings. Make our homes complete, and may your divine presence continue to dwell among us.

Grant us the merit to raise children and grandchildren who are wise and understanding, who love GOD and fear Him—men of truth, holy offspring—who cleave to GOD and who enlighten the world with Torah, the WORD of GOD, the Bible. With good deeds they work in the service of the Creator, the WORD, our LORD and Savior YASHUA HAMASHIAKH.

We now celebrate with You, and all of heaven, the seventh day of our rest, just as You rested from all Your work.

May we rejoice throughout this holy day and be refreshed and renewed in our bodies with Your strength, Your hope, Your joy and Your love.

We declare this by faith in YASHUA's name.

Amen.

FINAL REMARKS

Let's Review the 10 Commandments. Relate the letter to the commandment.

1. _____ **AHAVA (love)** opposite of **AF (anger)**
   Love THE LORD with all your heart . . .

2. _____ **BORE (Creator)** opposite **BIER (he destroyed)**
   Do not create any graven image.

3. _____ **GAAVTAN (vain)** reinforces **GOLEM (a fool)**
   Do not take the name of YAHWE in vain.

4. _____ **DEREKH (way)** opposite **DAKHA (to put off)**
   Remember the SHABAT.

5. _____ **HILEL (to praise)** opposite **HILLEL (Lucifer)**
   Honor your father and mother.

6. _____ **VAYIKRA (Legislation)** reinforces **VIDE (certify)**
   Do not kill.

7. _____ **ZAKUT (purity)** opposite **ZNUT (prostitution)**
   Do not commit adultery.

8. _____ **KHAMAD (lust, covet)** reinforces **KHET (sin)**
   Do not steal.

9. _____ **TUV (virtue)** opposite **TAUT (error)**
   Do not give false testimony against your neighbor.

10. _____ **YATSA (satisfied) opposite YIESH (to despair)**
    Do not covet . . .

The following book: **THE HEBREW ALPHABET, Pronunciation and Writing Exercises, Book 2** will teach you the next 11 letters of the Hebrew alphabet. These 11 letters will be relating to YASHUA's (Jesus') Decrees to Christians.

WORKS CONSULTED

Brown, Francis, S.R. Driver and Charles A. Briggs. *The Brown-Driver-Briggs Hebrew and English Lexicon*. Peabody, Massachusetts: Hendrickson Publishers, 2018.

Hayim, Baltsan. *Webster's New World Hebrew Dictionary*. New York: Macmillan General Reference, 1992.

Hebrew/English Translator. RustyBrick. Android app. 2010–2021.

Hebrew Interlinear Old Testament. Kyrshanlang R. Dkhar. Android app. 2019–2023.

Hebrew World English Bible. Bible Factory. Android app. 2017–2020.

QuickDic Dictionary. Reimar Döffinger. V. 5.6.3. Android app. 2015–2020.

Strong, James. *Strong's Exhaustive Concordance of the Bible with Greek and Hebrew Dictionaries*. Gordonsville, Tennessee: Dugan, 1980.

Torah: Holy Land Edition. Fort Worth, Texas: Zvi Zachor, 2015.

ANSWERS TO EXERCISES

BET, PAGE 7

ABA = אבא

GIMEL, PAGE 13

GAG = גג

DALET, PAGE 19

DAG = דג

HE, PAGE 25

HA = הא

AHAVA = אהבה

VAV, PAGE 31

HEVE = הוא

DAVID = דוד

ZAYIN, PAGE 37

ZUG = זוג

ZAHAV = זהב

KHET, PAGE 43

KHAGAG = חגג

KHAI = חי

TET, PAGE 49

TUV = טוב

TOV = טוב

TOVA = טובה

YOD, PAGE 55

YEHUDI = יהודי

YADA = ידה

YAD = יד

YAHWE = יהוה

GOI = גוי

KHAGIGA = חגיגה

EXERCISE 1, PAGE 61

אבא   ABA = Father

יד   YAD = hand

דג   DAG = fish

גג   GAG = roof

חגג   KHAGAG = to celebrate

דוד   DAVID = David

ידה   YADA = to praise, to worship

אהבה   AHAVA = love

EXERCISE 2, PAGE 61

My Father = AVI אבי

Good = TOV טוב

Hand = YAD יד

EXERCISE 3, PAGE 61

Father = ABA אבא

Behold = HE, HA הא

THE LORD = YAHWE יהוה

ABOUT THE AUTHOR

Silvia Owley was born in Mexico City in 1952. Her French mother was a trilingual interpreter for the United Nations and her Mexican father was the head of telecommunications in Mexico City. Her maternal grandfather was an American news reporter and photographer, and her French grandmother a foreign language teacher. Many cultures and creativity flowed into Silvia's blood preparing her *"for such a time as this"*.

Living in different countries forced her to adapt to new cultures and learn new languages. By age 12, she spoke Spanish, English and French, and studied German and Latin in school. She later became a trilingual secretary in Paris.

Not being a city dweller, she joined Club Med as a sports hostess when she turned 19 and worked in Martinique (Caribbean), then Tahiti. She excelled in scuba diving, tennis, ping pong—as outdoors activities were her Paradise—not being in an office.

She married at age 23 and lived in Squaw Valley, California where she became a snow-ski instructor. She has two daughters and a grandson, and is living today in Florida with her husband, Roger, both loving the game of golf.

Living in California, then Nevada, she formed Silvia's Language Services, Inc., and later, Silvia's Language Ministries, Inc. Hundreds of students benefited from learning the basics for reading, writing then speaking these foreign languages.

In 2014, while attending a Messianic church, she became fascinated by the Hebrew symbols and determined to master the Hebrew language. Seeking guidance from the Holy Spirit, she was led to study Hebrew just like she taught other foreign languages—step by step, letter by letter, sound by sound, repetition and memorization. After years of hard work, she achieved her desired goal. Today Silvia can read, write, translate and even sing Hebrew prayers.

To contact the author, email royallyeducated@gmail.com